THE MAGIC MOMENT

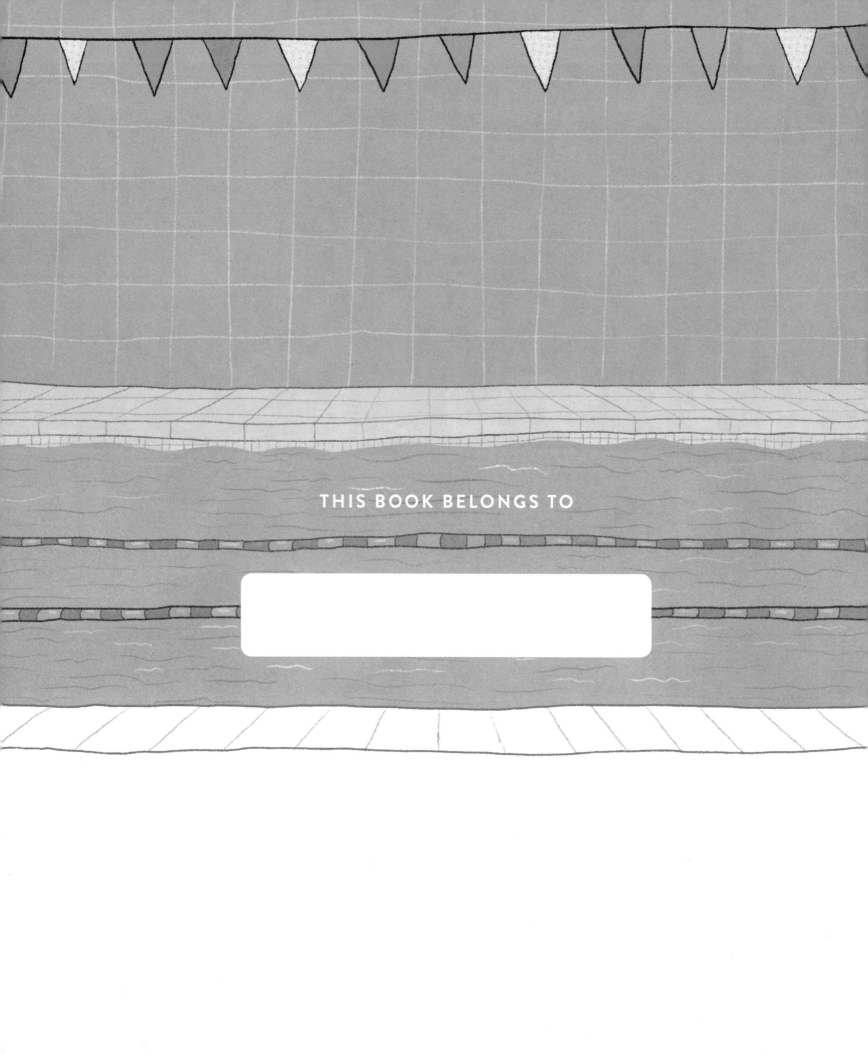

THIS BOOK BELONGS TO

Items should be returned on or before the date shown below. Items not already requested by other borrowers may be renewed in person, in writing or by telephone. To renew, please quote the number on the barcode label. To renew online a PIN is required. This can be requested at your local library. DCPL9000078416
Renew online @ www.dublincitypubliclibraries.ie
Fines charged for overdue items will include postage incurred in recovery.
Damage to or loss of items will be charged to the borrower.

Leabharlanna Poiblí Chathair Bhaile Átha Cliath
Dublin City Public Libraries

Due Date	Due Date	Due Date

THE MAGIC MOMENT

NIALL BRESLIN

ILLUSTRATED BY SHEENA DEMPSEY

GILL BOOKS

Gill Books

Hume Avenue

Park West

Dublin 12

www.gillbooks.ie

Gill Books is an imprint of M.H. Gill and Co.

Text © Niall Breslin 2018
Illustrations © Sheena Dempsey 2018
978 07171 8133 9

Designed by www.grahamthew.com
Printed by L.E.G.O. SpA, Italy

This book is typeset in 16pt pn 21pt Archer Medium
The paper used in this book comes from the wood pulp of managed forests.
For every tree felled, at least one tree is planted, thereby renewing natural
resources.

5 4 3 2 1

FOREWORD

What I love about this book is that it teaches children a really simple and effective mindfulness technique, which they can bring with them anywhere they go, for managing their big feelings. The 'magic moment' technique works by anchoring a child to the present moment by using the power of their breath, a happy thought and squeezing their fingers tight, which makes 'their magic moment shine so bright'.

The beauty of mindfulness is that it allows children to increase awareness of their full range of experience, including their thoughts, feelings and bodily sensations, without becoming overwhelmed by them. Research indicates that mindfulness helps children to manage negative feelings like fear, sadness and anger, and improves their self-esteem and overall well-being. When children learn to be more 'present' in the moment, they can pay better attention and make wiser decisions. In this modern-day busy age, mindfulness is a crucial life skill for us all, and the earlier we introduce it to children the more prepared they will be to grow into emotionally healthy adults.

When we teach mindfulness to children, it engages all their senses and turns it into a fun activity. *The Magic Moment* does just this with its playful and catchy rhyme, making it all the more memorable for children and adults alike. I will definitely be reading this book with my own children and the children that I see, and I can envisage it being incorporated into schools as a powerful self-help tool to boost children's emotional well-being and develop their resilience skills.

Dr Malie Coyne, Clinical Psychologist and NUIG Lecturer

A NOTE FOR PARENTS

When I was a kid, my mum used to tell me I was a worrier. That was her nice way of explaining why I welded myself to her leg whenever we went out, or called her in the middle of the night to pick me up if I was staying in a friend's house because I was 'sick'.

As kids, and I suppose even as adults, we are custom made to avoid things that make us sad, scared or unsettled, and to seek out things that make us happy, excited and content. It's as if the world values our shiny, happier feelings but turns a blind eye to our (very normal) painful feelings. Oh, if life were so easy.

The reality is that no one navigates their way through life without facing obstacles, fears and difficult times, yet we perceive negative emotions as something we should avoid at all costs, rather than something we should explore, accept and deal with. This is instilled in us from early childhood and tends to stay with us throughout our lives.

Noticing your child's emotions and reflecting them with empathy can help your child understand that it's OK to experience all feelings and to talk about them. Exploring mindfulness techniques that allow children to express themselves and recognise that they can work with rather than against these emotions empowers their sense of self when dealing with fear, sadness and anger. Their curiosity and open minds already cultivate the very foundations of mindfulness, making them perfect students.

Children these days deal with a lot. The world is moving very fast and can feel really overwhelming to them sometimes. When I was six years old, I was eating worms covered in muck in the garden, and the world beyond my back garden and house didn't exist for me. Now kids take in so much information that they are often pulled from the present moment continually throughout their day – it's a sensory overload for their young brains, from which mindful techniques can provide respite.

Creating a mindful space for kids to recognise how truly amazing they are is one of the best gifts you can give them, and one which will stay with them throughout their lives. I really hope *The Magic Moment* helps you and your child to take the first step in that direction. I wish I'd known this trick when I was a kid.

Bressie

Freddie stood at the end of his mum and dad's bed,
wearing the new swimming gear they had bought him.

'Is it time to go swimming yet?' he asked.

'Not for another few hours, Freddie,'
said his very sleepy mum.

Freddie lay on the floor and practised his swimming stroke.
Today, for the first time, he would be swimming in a real pool!

'Come and eat your breakfast, Freddie. Even little dinosaurs need energy,' laughed his mum.

Freddie felt too excited to eat, but his mum had made his favourite breakfast.

Freddie's dad said he had to wait a whole hour after his breakfast before he could go swimming.

It felt like forever ...

So, while he waited, Freddie helped his dad pack the swimming bag.

Dinosaur armbands? CHECK!

Swimming togs? CHECK!

Towel? CHECK!

But where were his goggles?

When they arrived at the pool, Freddie rushed into the
changing room. There were lots of bigger boys there.
They were very loud and excited, too.

Suddenly, Freddie's tummy felt a bit funny.
He didn't feel quite so keen to jump in.

'It's too cold, Dad. I don't want to go swimming today.'

'It's OK, Freddie,' said his dad gently. 'You will warm up in no time.'

'No, Dad. I just want to go home,' said Freddie.

Freddie felt really sad that he was too afraid to get into the water. He was sorry he didn't get the chance to use all the cool swimming gear his mum and dad had bought him.

'Don't worry. We'll go again another day and you'll be fine. You'll like it once you get used to it,' said his dad.

But Freddie had decided he was never going back. It was too scary.

That night one of Freddie's favourite people came to visit.
Nana always had time to read him stories and sing songs.

Nana asked Freddie about his trip to the pool, so he told her he had been too afraid to get in.

'It's OK to feel scared, Freddie,' said Nana.

'Really, Nana?' he replied with surprise.

'Would you like me to teach you a very special trick that you can use every time you feel a bit scared or sad?'

Freddie's eyes lit up. 'Yes please, Nana!'

While Nana helped Freddie get ready for bed, she explained the trick.

'Close your eyes and think of the happiest, most fun day you can remember.'

Freddie had so many happy memories that he wasn't sure which one to choose.

He thought of the cool
new bike he got on
Christmas Day ...

... and the time he went
to the fun park and won
his dinosaur teddy.

But the happiest, most fun day in the whole world was the day he got his dog, Larry. He thought about Larry jumping up and licking his face and chasing him all over the house!

They had played all day until they both fell asleep
under the apple tree that Freddie's dad had planted
for him when he was born.

'I've got my happy memory, Nana!' said Freddie.

'OK, Freddie. Now squeeze your thumb and finger on each hand together really tight. Take ten deep breaths and keep thinking about that magic moment. And always remember ...

When you're scared or feeling sad
A little bit angry, a little bit mad

Just slow down and start to breathe
In and out ten times with ease

Think of something that makes you smile
And hold the thought for a little while

Then squeeze your fingers really tight
And your magic moment will shine so bright'

Freddie woke up the next morning feeling much better.

He thought about how sad he felt coming home from the pool, but then he thought about the new trick Nana taught him.

The magic moment had worked!

Maybe he would give swimming one more try after all.

When Freddie went back to the pool with
his dad, the big, noisy boys were there again.

He put his thumbs and fingers together, closed his eyes
and took ten deep breaths, just like Nana had taught him.

'What are you up to, munchkin?' asked his dad.

'I'm just doing my magic moment trick.'

Freddie stood at the side of the pool. He took a
deep breath, held his nose and ...

SPLASH! He jumped right in.

And that was the most magical moment of all.

I hope you enjoyed this story. Freddie found the pool really scary the first time he went, didn't he? There are many times I have felt scared and sad but that's OK – it happens to everyone, you know! The next time you feel scared or sad like Freddie, why don't you try the Magic Moment Trick for yourself?

Bressie x

•

THE MAGIC MOMENT TRICK

When you're scared or feeling sad
A little bit angry, a little bit mad

Just slow down and start to breathe
In and out ten times with ease

Think of something that makes you smile
And hold the thought for a little while

Then squeeze your fingers really tight
And your magic moment will shine so bright

•